In this book, Alex, Ben, Jo and Rusty want to solve some science puzzles. They all have different ideas. Can you help them answer their questions?

What do YOU think about our ideas? Do you have any other ideas? Why don't you talk to someone about what you think?

We'll show you how we try to find out the answers. You can try to find out too!

Alex

Ben

A note to adults ▶

This book shows children that science is everywhere, and that they can find out about the world for themselves by thinking and investigating.

You can help children by reading the book with them and asking questions. At the start of each story, talk about what the characters are saying. While children are investigating, you could ask: What is happening? What can you see? Why do you think this is happening? Is it what you expected to happen? Children should be supervised while they are doing the investigations.

Each story ends with a simple explanation of what has happened. There are ideas for follow-up activities at the back of the book, and children may also want to find out more from other books, CD-Roms or the Internet.

Text copyright © 2000 Brenda and Stuart Naylor
Illustrations copyright © 2000 Ged Mitchell

Designed by Sarah Borny
Edited by Anne Clark

The rights of Brenda and Stuart Naylor and Ged Mitchell to be identified
as the authors and artist of this work have been asserted.

First published in 2000 by Hodder Children's Books,
a division of Hodder Headline,
338 Euston Road, London NW1 3BH

10 9 8 7 6 5 4 3 2 1

ISBN 0340 75754 X Hardback
ISBN 0340 75755 8 Paperback
Printed in Hong Kong

The Snowman's Coat
and other **science** questions ▶

Brenda and Stuart Naylor

Illustrated by Ged Mitchell

Hodder Children's Books

a division of Hodder Headline

The Snowman's ✳ Coat

It is a winter's day. It has been snowing outside. Rusty, Jo and Alex are making a snowman. They want to stop him melting in the sun.

Don't put the coat on the snowman. He'll melt!

Ben will help you investigate.

▶ Fill two empty yoghurt pots with water.

② ▶ Put them in the freezer until the water has turned into ice.

▶ You have made two snowmen. Turn them out of the pots and put them on a tray.

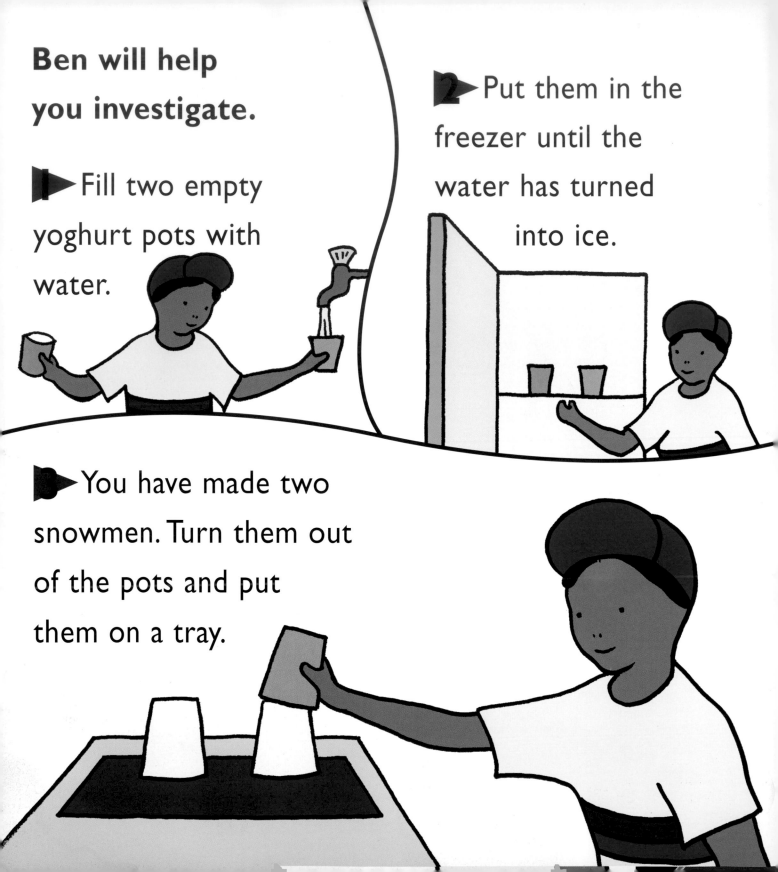

4▶ Make a coat for one snowman. You could use an old sock or a cloth.

5▶ Wait a while and see which snowman melts first.

What did you find out? ▶

The coat does not make the snowman warmer. It just keeps him at the same temperature for longer. So the coat will make the snowman last longer.

The Sailing Boat

Alex, Ben and Rusty are at the pond. They want to sail their new boat across the middle of the pond.

Don't let the boat go too far out. It will sink in the deep water.

Jo will help you investigate.

1 ▶ Find a deep bowl and fill it halfway up with water.

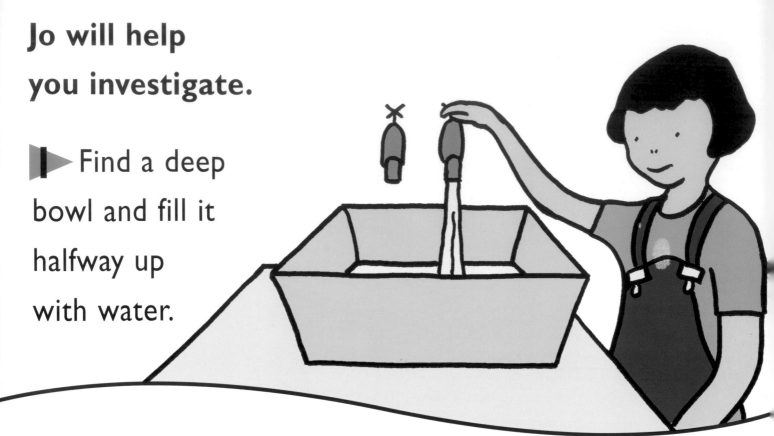

2 ▶ Float a boat in the water. You could use an empty margarine tub.

3 Pour some more water into the bowl.

4 See how the boat floats now. Does the deeper water make a difference?

What did you find out?

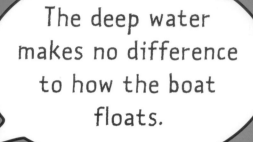

Boats are made to float well. They will float in shallow water or deep water, so it doesn't matter how far out the boat goes. It will still float.

A Shady Spot

It's a sunny day. The sun is very hot. Auntie Liz is sitting in the shadow of a tree. She has fallen asleep in the shade.

Alex will help you investigate.

▶ Put a stick in the ground on a sunny day.

2 ▶ Mark where the shadow is and then leave it for an hour.

3 See if the shadow is in the same place as it was.

What did you find out?

Shadows don't stay in the same place all day. The sun appears to move during the day. The shadows move as well.

Icy Drinks

Jo, Ben and Alex have put lots of ice in their drinks. They find that there is water on the outside of the glasses. They are wondering where the water has come from.

Look! The water is oozing out through the sides of the glass.

Rusty will help you investigate.

1 ▶ Get three glasses.

2 ▶ Put some warm water in one glass and leave it.

3 ▶ Put ice in the next glass and put a saucer over the top of the glass.

4 ▶ Put ice in the third glass.

5 ▷ Leave them all on a tray for a while and see if any of the glasses are wet on the outside.

What did you find out? ▷

There is water in the air that we can't see. This water can form into drops on cold things. We can see it when it forms into drops. We call the drops condensation.

Now you have started finding out, you might not want to stop!

The Snowman's Coat

Can you find other ways to make snow or ice last longer? Why not try other materials such as newspaper and polystyrene? Does the thickness of the material make a difference?

The Sailing Boat

Can you think of other things that might affect the way a boat floats? See if it makes a difference how many people are in the boat. Does the colour of the boat make a difference? What if the water is salty, like the sea?

A Shady Spot

Go outside to look at different shadows. Look at the shadows several times during the day. Do they move? Do they all move in the same direction? Does the same thing happen the next sunny day?

Icy Drinks

Where else can you see condensation? Try the bathroom and the kitchen. Have a look at cars on a cold morning. Look at someone's glasses when they come indoors on a very cold day.

Have fun finding out more!